RELEASING THE WHY

Releasing the Why

Library of Congress Cataloging-in-Publication Data
Name: Henderson-Williams, Gladys
Title: Releasing the Why

ISBN 9780578631226

Published by GHW Productions LLC
2019 Cunningham Dr., Ste. 416
Hampton, VA 23666
www.manifestdestiny.com

Dedication

In dedication to the sweet memories shared with a wonderful man.

December 19, 2019 is your 4th birthday away from me. When the month of December started, I knew I'd have to face December 19th. I tried everything I knew to prepare myself for this day. I recited every strength scripture I could remember from Dec 1st - Dec 18th. When I opened my eyes on Dec 19th, the loneliness was greater than all my preparation. And just as the cover picture depicts, you quietly slipped away. The footprints you left can never be filled. Your legacy is forever preserved. My heart hurts every day that I awake and realize you are not in our bed. Today was no different.

To my beloved husband, Andrew Williams Sr., I miss you each and every day. You took flight on May 31, 2016 to be with God. You supported me with great love, protection, and lots of understanding. You believed in me and when I wanted to give up or give in to stresses and fear, you would stop whatever you were doing to pray for me. I still need you. I need you more than ever to help me navigate through this season of my life. I ask myself everyday 'what would Andrew do?' And some days I ask myself WHY?

Introduction

The WHYS in my life will never end. The emotional state of my life somedays is like a massive jigsaw puzzle. When you begin to put a puzzle together, you're taught to put the edges together first. The frame of the puzzle creates a boundary for which all the other pieces will fit perfectly. The boarder pieces of the puzzle are easy to identify because they have flat edges.

This is also the way we've sometimes framed our lives. We identify our boarders, lock the pieces neatly together then spend the rest of our life trying to fit the pieces together to look like the picture on the top of the box - in our minds.

We constantly look at the box top of the puzzle to remind us of the beautiful tapestry that we can display to the world when it is finished.

We identify pieces of the puzzle that we think will build a segment of the picture. If there's a tree in the picture, we carefully pick all the puzzle pieces that are the color of the tree. We get excited because of the plan we have to put the puzzle together in segments. The same as in life, we come up with a plan to devise steps to achieve our life goals. The pieces start to fit neatly into place – this gives us hope.

Isn't it amazing how little accomplishments give us GREAT hope? Our spirit is renewed and revived. We're on our way to greater accomplishments. We look at the jigsaw puzzle and say 'this is easy' only to look at the box top and see there's a part of the puzzle that has the sky with clouds and the different shades of blue has caused you to rethink our confession of 'this is easy'.

The calm seasons in our lives have caused us to make the same statement about life 'this is easy'. We believe that we have this thing call life all figured out and we're decreeing and declaring to the world 'this is easy.'

Then one day an unbearable situation occurs, and it hits so hard that you don't know how to respond. It could be something small, but because you figured that life is easy – the situation will seem insurmountable. And just like the jigsaw puzzle with the different shades of blue with the clouds we go from 'this is easy' to why has this happened? Why wasn't I ready for this storm to hit. Why didn't I see this coming? I should have been prepared. Why is life so hard and unpredictable? I really thought I was living 'my best life' by demonstrating to the world that I'm strong and courageous. My superman shield has taken a hit and pieces of my shield have come off and my shield doesn't fit my body anymore. Just like the puzzle, the frame of the shield is still intact, but the inside pieces of the shield have been rearranged.

Mind you that all the pieces of the puzzle are still available to complete the beautiful picture that the box top shows, it's just I can't seem to identify the pieces that connect together as easily as I'd envisioned. My life has taken major hit and I can't, for the life of me, pull my sanity back in alignment. I struggle to get back to the season of my life where things were calm, so I ask God WHY?

Table of Contents

Why Why Why 11

Why Not 27

Why That Answer.....................................33

What's Holding You....................................45

Why Release the Why 55

Release 60

Acknowledgement 75

Chapter One

Why~Why~Why

It has taken me several years to bring myself to this point to make the decision to address 'releasing the WHYs' in my life regarding many of the events that have taken a toll on me. I've always been an inquisitive person from my childhood to this very tender age of 65. If something didn't make sense to me, I'd ask why. An inquisitive person can drive you insane! Yes, I've probably added to the list of people who are insane because of my inquisitiveness. The word WHY lends itself to demanding a response. From my point of view, I find asking why not to be an imposition. Let's dig into the definition of the word WHY-

- Noun – a reason or explanation
- Adverb – for what reason or purpose
- Exclamation – used to add emphasis to a response

None of these definitions are intimidating. So, when asked WHY by someone, either respond with a truthful answer or respond with – I don't know the answer to your why. If you ever have a conversation with a five-year-old and make the statement 'you can't have a cookie before dinner' – the first word out of the five-year-old's mouth is WHY? When you try to respond with a logical answer to a five-year-old, it will not work because they will continue until your response becomes, 'because I said so' and that's not polite. But how many times have you used this response to end a never-ending conversation just about a cookie before dinner. That one word is learned at a young age and we carry it throughout our teen, young adult and adult life and use it on repeat – WHY? We spend much of our life asking humans WHY, but we were taught it was a lack of faith to ask our creator WHY.

Growing up in a Christian home, I was taught never to question God and any of His actions. It was as if you didn't have faith or trust God, and you just had to live with whatever happened in your life. Over my 60+ years of living, I thought to question God was going against everything that I'd been taught by my God-fearing parents and because I never wanted to disappoint them, I lived in this state of wanting answers that no earthly person could answer for me. Believe me I tried to have many conversations with individuals who I thought could speak on God's behalf just to give me one answer that I could rest all my WHYs. I never approached any of the 'close to God' people with a blunt question like 'Why would God, Why did God'...because I feared they believed that it was wrong to question God. I had to be discreet in my endeavor to get just one 'WHY' answered.

Because I didn't want to appear to have a lack of faith, I went to the Bible and my trusted Strong's Concordance and discovered the word WHY is used 163 time in the Old Testament, 98 times in the New Testament and 23 times in the Apocrypha. Let's brake from this discovery and explain the Apocrypha. Apocrypha are books included in the Septuagint and Vulgate but excluded from the Jewish and Protestant canons of the Old Testament and early Christian writings not included in the New

Testament. Did you know that there are books that were written but not included in the Old or New Testament? This is a great topic for your next Bible Study.

I'm not so naive to believe that I will get all the answers to my life's issues before I leave this earth, but to live with this great desire to know WHY things happen in my life can easily become tormenting. When I've spent the better part of my life feeling that I had no faith if I asked God for answers to things that hurt me...come on!!!! I was being tormented with FEAR, being tormented to feel I could ask God for health, wealth, food, material things and HE would deliver them, but could not ask HIM WHY. This somehow felt like living in an abusive relationship where you had to live on guard and say the right things or you would be ex-communicated from your salvation. Your life may have been very sweet and lovely without any reason to want to ask God WHY. Well that's not my testimony. If like me you've wanted to know the answer to an event that has happened in your life and you knew only God had the answer, then keep reading.

We see devastations in the news of a child being molested and we say 'why didn't someone see this coming' we see flooding in our nation and some people don't evacuate and we say 'why didn't they leave when they saw the weather changing?' We see incidents happen in our own homes and we ask 'why did you do this or that?' Not only do we ask WHY, but we wait for an answer or we go to our trusted advisor Google to explore human behavior across our nation and in our home. Why do I use Google – because somewhere in the universe, someone has asked the same question, or someone has written a commentary on the same subject. Whether the Google answer is true or false, we tend to find some sort of calmness that satisfies our inquisitiveness. Isn't it amazing how getting a quick response, whether it is true of false will give us a peace of mind? Is it because the response came quick and we didn't have to pray, fast and/or wait on a response, Selah.

Jeremiah 33:3 - Call to Me and I will answer you, and I will tell you great and mighty things, which you do not know (NASB). WOW. We have become a microwave society where we want everything to be an instant. When I say microwave society, think back to before the microwave came into existence and you wanted a homemade baked potato, you knew that the only way to get a homemade baked potato, was to put it in the oven. Putting it in the oven took time for the potato to cook to the desired softness. According to Google, to bake a medium size potato in the oven it takes 1 hour to 1.5 hours, in the microwave it only takes 5 minutes. Some people have argued over the years that the potato baked in the oven has a better texture than the potato baked in the microwave – I don't get into those discussions, because every fast food joint has a baked potato that I can get through the drive thru. This analogy is neither right or wrong and not the only answer. However, in Jeremiah 33:3 when God says Call to me and I will answer, it's God's promise to mankind. But here is a point that I've experienced, God said that He would answer, but HE didn't say when He would answer. This is the part that has caused me my greatest discomfort.

Discomfort in the sense of wanting an answer from God immediately. I can admit that there have been times that God answered my partition immediately. Then there are times that my faith has been tested to wait for an answer. There have been times that I convinced myself that God had answered my prayer, just to satisfy my flesh and move out in a direction that caused me greater issues. You may have never experienced this — but I have. Only to realize, that had I waited on God to answer, it would have saved me many sleepless nights. When I have gone ahead of God's response, I had to spend a lot of time fixing what I messed up. It's a tough place to reside in when you force the answer your flesh wants and not wait on God's perfect will. It's amazing how many times I've found myself repenting repeatedly because I didn't wait on God to answer. It's amazing how many times I've quoted, I have faith, I trust God's timing for my life...yeah right. Have you ever asked God for an answer to a life issue and felt that you had waited long enough and that you could figure it out on your own? If you haven't then don't start now. Many times, I've prayed and asked God for help and then turned around and convinced myself that I had enough word in me to not bother God with this little issue and just go fix things myself. I used a lot of energy reasoning with God because I was taught not to ask Him WHY things were so chaotic. There's that word again that I was taught to never ask God – WHY!

So, this statement to Jeremiah is still relevant today, but I believe even those Christians who won't confess this to be true in public, from the pulpit, bible study and prayer meetings, are privately asking God

WHY. If you're brave enough to have a WHY conversation, the most spiritual person will immediately jump to 1 Corinthians 13:12 - For now we see through a glass, darkly; but then face to face: *now I know in part*; but then shall I know even as also I am known."

This is not the answer to the WHY questions. This scripture is specifically talking about the Excellence of Love – not the 'don't ever ask God Why?' I've witnessed the Bible being the most misused book that I have ever seen. It is dangerous to put the Bible in the hands of a well-versed person with a great memory - one who can quote scriptures who is without understanding and the leading of the Holy Spirit. 2 Timothy 2:15 says (you) Study to shew thyself approved unto God, a workman that needeth not to be ashamed, **rightly dividing the word of truth,** KJV.

When the word of God is not rightly divided but used as a baseball bat to beat people into man's interpretation and use of scripture, it is wrong. It is so important to study the word of God under the leading of the Holy Spirit to get the correct meaning of the scripture so you can rightly divide the word of God.

The majority of my life has been surrounded by church folks. Traditional church folks – saved people who study the word of God and are amazing teachers of the word of God. I learned a lot from sitting in Sunday School, Baptist Training Union, Vacation Bible School, my daddy's preaching and some amazing pastors that I've been pastored by. As I stated earlier, I grew up in a Christian home. I love sitting in a bible study where the word of God is taught. I said all of that to say that I don't ever remember anyone explaining how to get the answer to my WHY questions. Here are a few of my WHY questions – only a few. I have many more

- Why do bad things happen to saved people?
- Why do some saved Christians suffer diseases for long periods of time before dying?
- Why do babies suffer abuse at the hands of their biological parents?
- Why are Christians not allowed to grieve in the house of the Lord?
- If a saved person shows emotions at the homegoing of their loved one, Why it is perceived as a lack of faith?
- If a saved person smiles two weeks after the death of a loved, Why it is perceived by church folks that there was no love for the loved one?

- Why is it perceived that every single person in the church is looking for a spouse?

- Why did God come get my mama when I was so young?

- Why did God allow my sister, brother, mother or father to become addicted to drugs?

- Why is forgiving so hard?

- Why am I not living the abundant life God promised?

- Why are my children so rebellious and I'm living for God?

- Why does it seem that many churches are not winning souls?

- Why have churches moved away from true Bible Study...where are the teachers?

- WHY – WHY-- WHY .... So many WHYs in my life. What do I do? How

many WHYs do you have in your
life?

Can you imagine having to live with so many
WHYs? I'm not confronted with all of these
at the same time, but my list seems to have
grown with the events that I've experienced
over my 60+ years. Then you may say,
you've served the Lord for many years, true.
You were raised in a Christian home, true.
You've studied the word of God from
childhood, true. You were raised in a home
with your biological mother and father, true.
You were a Sunday School, Vacation Bible
School teacher, Musician, Choir Director,
true. You served as a department leader,
Elder and Associate Pastor, true. So, your
question to me is probably - how have you
been able to love, witness, serve God and
allow your list of WHYs to grow so long?
Glad you asked – because I felt only God
had the answers and when I get to heaven

my WHYs wouldn't matter any longer. If I could just hold on (suffer through) to all my WHYs, I'd be okay in the end. There you have the answer. I was never a disrespectful child and believed that if I could hold on (suffer through with my why and never question God) then I would never be a disappointment to my parents. So, I held true to their teachings. Now at my tender age of 65, I've come to understand that my parents taught what they knew and what they had been taught. Right, wrong or indifferent – I love and respect their rearing of us their children.

Chapter Two

WHY Not

The word WHY is not a bad word nor does is it carry a negative connotation. I've met people who believe by asking WHY, you're challenging their intellect. When someone ask you a question beginning with the word WHY, most of the time they are asking for a greater understanding of the statement you just made. I've seen where some individuals become irate because someone asked 'WHY'. You see, I've been that person on many occasions. In giving a briefing to a company of people I have been challenged from the audience with a WHY?

27

Well, my inside voice response is 'because I said so, now sit down, be quiet and stop trying to be seen'. Go ahead and raise your hand and repeat after me 'I've done the same thing', maybe not in a briefing setting but with my family and friends, especially with my children.

I've discovered that I only became offended when I couldn't answer the 'WHY'. There were times in my career that I spoke to large audiences and thought I'd communicated the topic of the presentation quite clearly. Only to discover that it was clear to me but clear as mud to the audience. I found that being asked 'WHY' in a group setting can cause you to do more research on the topic, or cause you to look from a different perspective that you'd not explored.

Another reason is someone really wanting to make you look dumb. There are those....

Here's something I want you observe when watching a person being interviewed on television. The interviewer is seeking to get answers to questions that he or she believes will expose something about the person that will raise the viewing audience. The interviewer will always have a 'gotcha question' in their list to be asked. When the interviewer asks a very pointed questions the person being interviewed will respond 'that's a good question' – this is a brain pause for the person being interviewed to formulate a response. If the person being interviewed is expecting a 'gotcha question' their response is 'I'm glad you asked'. It's always funny to me to watch interviews because what the interviewer is really asking is 'WHY' do you believe what you believe?

The word WHY has made many people that we know and read about very successful:

- Henry Ford – we have horse drawn carriages, WHY build a Model-T a car

- Wright Brothers - we have cars, WHY build an airplane

- William Bell – what is a telephone and WHY do we need it

- Martin Cooper – invented the first cellular phone. WHY a cellular phone

- Charles Cabbage – created the first computer. Why a computer

- Steve Jobs – revolutionized computer, cellular phone, iPad, iPhone

- Madam CJ Walker – invented African American hair products. Why?

Because she suffered from a scalp ailment that cause her own hair loss

These are just a few successful individuals who were challenged to answer the question 'WHY'.

Don't become afraid to ask WHY in the right connotation. I'm challenged in my life constantly asking myself WHY did I make that decision, WHY am I responding this way, WHY haven't I taken more time to research an issue before becoming offended. There are times I've become offended with myself for not asking for additional information. If we are afraid to ask 'WHY' to gain greater understanding, then we find ourselves working overtime to convince ourselves to believe that we know the answer...counseling with ourselves can be dangerous in some instances. Let go of pride, or the appearance of feeling inadequate, or ignorant and respectfully ask 'WHY'. This is a personal testimony! I will also testify to not being so respectful at time when screaming to God 'WHY' have you forsaken me?

Reflect on times when you've had to ask the question 'WHY' to people and to God and you received a greater understand of the topic. As you reflect begin to write your testimony in this book.

Chapter Three

Why That Answer

God says to Call to me, and I will answer you. The definition of call is a cry made as a summons or to attract someone's attention. The word call is found 142 times in the Old Testament, 47 times in the New Testament and 26 times in the Apocrypha. My small understanding of this is to call for HELP! God said to call to HIM not anyone else in this passage of scripture...so I called unto God and he heard me. I made my partition to Him in the form of a question WHY are so many things, that I perceive to be devasting, are happening to me. I asked the question from a personal standpoint because the things that were happening were affecting me, I was disappointed and hurting really bad. As humans, we've been taught to ask our questions to the person who has the answers, so I asked God because no other earthly human had any answers to my WHY. As I'm sitting at my desk writing, I believe in my spirit that God has answered many of my WHY's and because I didn't like the answer, I kept going back to HIM in hopes that He would give me the answer I wanted to hear. But do I know what answer I wanted to hear? I know in my heart that God is probably saying, spend more time in my word, spend more time thanking me, spend more time giving of yourself to help others and stop sitting around waiting on an answer that you're not ready to handle. Asking for that specific answer can sometimes cause problems for you in areas of your being such as insomnia, overeating, anger, lack of trust, not eating, anxiousness, impatience, wanting to be at home, then not wanting to be home-definitely didn't want to be around people these were just a few of my battles. I mention these areas because I'm a first partaker of each of these. Each time I experienced the loss of a loved one, these areas would come back to visit and set up camp around and in me. I was being tormented and felt no one would understand. I wanted to talk with someone, but the lack of trusting anyone drove me into seclusion. Have you ever gone through a tough time in your life, needed to talk with a trusted friend and felt 'I definitely can't tell anyone about this one?' Join me in singing

'We shall Overcome – SOMEDAY' I want to overcome believing that I can trust someone to hear my heart and walk with me just for a little while until I'm strong enough to do this on my own. Yes, I'm surrounded by people who love me all the time but am I comfortable enough to relax and release? You may be experiencing or have experienced this same thing. Sometimes in my self-talk sessions, I convince myself (for 10 seconds) that I can trust a certain individual with part of my inward struggles and even say to myself – the next time I see them, I'm going to release some of this weight off me and maybe they can give me sound advice. I build myself up to go forth. Guess what happens when the opportunity presents itself – the enemy tells me; you can't expose yourself like that. Now here's the thing that convinces me that I can't relax and release. When my sisters and I were growing up, my Dad would say to us things that were meant to mold us into independent adult ladies.

- There are only two kinds of people in the world when it comes to your problems. First, people who are glad you have a problem and second, people who are glad it's not their problem
- No man wants a crying, whining, and complaining woman

Now can you imagine hearing these statement as a child from your Dad/hero? It was important to me to be obedient to my Dad/hero. So, I took it to heart, and I took it into adulthood and made it a big part of my survival kit. I took it into every relationship with people who wanted to befriend me, work, church, and personal. It was the fortress that I built for myself. It's the fortress I built, not God. I convinced myself that it was the safest place for me to reside – me and God, honoring my Dad.

To this day, I can hear my Dad repeating these phrases. I'm sure that there are sayings that your parent or guardians have said to you as a child, that you still remember, reverence and live by to this present day. These were not only the phrases that he instilled in us, but it's statements like this, when taken out of context that can be detrimental to living free. Just a little bit about my Dad, Rev Paul. He was a pastor, strong presence in the community with government officials, influencer, encourager, successful entrepreneur owning a construction company, ultimate provider and was adopted by a white family at the age of twelve. My dad was born September 2, 1897 and I can't begin to imagine what life was like for him being raised by white parents in the early 1900s. He enlisted in the US Army in 1915 and was honorably discharged in 1919. He only shared bits and pieces with us about his childhood, but apparently the sayings he made to us came from somewhere in his growing up years. He never showed affection, neither hugging us nor telling us that he loved us. However, he was the ultimate provider. We always lived in large brick homes, on lots of land that included a pond stocked with fish that my mom could fish in while he worked out of town. We always had at least three cars, a motorcycle, and even a school bus. There were three gardens with lots of vegetables, a field with hog, cows, chickens and fruit trees. Literally, every material thing we needed was available on our land. This was his way of showing that he loved us. Every task, chore was made into a competition with him. Looking back now, Irealize that he could only give what he knew and what he had received. It breaks my heart when I think about him not being raised with love and affection.

I'm writing this portion to remind me and you that we need to be mindful of what we say to our children and our children's children that will be carried into their adulthood. Whether we're parenting them from a place of brokenness in our own life or affirming them by using the word of God to send them out into the world whole. Selah moment.

Taking what my Dad had instilled in us from childhood, were the bricks I used to erect many barricades of protections for myself. I disregarded people who God had sent into my life that I could confide in and relax in their presence. I was so consumed with protecting myself that I literally pushed people away. I know God was probably saying 'I'm send her answers to her prayers through human form, but she's not receiving the way I'm answering'. I was stubborn and hardheaded on receiving help from God because help didn't come the way I wanted it to come. I had my own vision of what help looked like. When we pray and ask for help, we don't get to choose what help looks like. I wanted that one person that I could just dump everything on and hope to feel better/lighter and let them deal with my issues while I lived a free life.

I was attending a Bible institute class and this lady, a new member to our church, came to me after a class and said, 'God told me that I was to learn from you, that you are Paul and I'm Timothy' – I truly wish I had an emoji to insert right here what my face looked like upon hearing this. I kindly smiled and said ok. In my heart, I was saying 'I'm NOBODY's Paul get away from me lady'. This was the last thing I wanted to be tasked to do. This would help for my present and future that I didn't want to accept because it came with a task. Why this lady, why not someone who I was familiar with? This relationship proved to be the God ordained relationship that I would need, love, and treasure for the rest of my life. I'm blessed beyond measure because of our relationship. The roles have switched, I'm Timothy and she is Paul.

I had a very bad habit of praying and asking God for answers, and after praying, sitting and painting the picture of how I thought He would answer. I wanted all my answers from God to be the way I had envisioned. God was answering all the time, but it was me saying 'Why that answer?'

When you pray and ask God for help, don't allow yourself to be so stuck in the vision of what you think the answer will be.

Try this process

- Pray
- Ask God for Grace to accept the way HE will answer
- Rest in what you prayed

- Be open to how HE answers
- Trust that HE knows best

Chapter Four

_W_hat's _H_olding _Y_ou

Let's look into the definition of confinement – confine to keep or restrict someone within certain limits, to restrain or forbid someone for leaving. Confinement? Most people I know would never consider volunteering themselves for confinement. To even think about being in a state of confinement makes me tremble. I think of confinement as a prison, a jail cell with no freedom. If you've ever looked at a movie that shows a prison, we always see someone in a small concrete area with a door that someone else has the key to. Someone else determines when you eat and sleep, they watch you to remind you that you are trapped until they make the decision to give you freedom. There is no sunshine in your confined area. We see in movies that depict a prison cell, that good behavior and time served will get you the possibility of going before a warden for early release, this is called parole. The opportunity to be set free. The warden in my confinement of being afraid to ask God WHY, was the enemy of my soul. He tormented me with feelings that I would be a disappointment to my parents and be ousted from the circle of faith-filled believers. He used every tactic that I held dear to keep me confined. I fell for his tricks many times. Here's what I'd say 'Forgive me Mama and Daddy for going against what you've taught, but I need to ask God a few

WHYs.' That would last until I got my mind ready to have the conversation with God and a picture of me seeing my parents crying would pop up and I'd just say, I'll try again on another day. The enemy, that joker, is persistent. The enemy wants to keep us in confinement because he likes control and power. I was giving him too much authority over my freedom. He was so smooth in his manipulation that I fell for it every time. From a child, we've been shown a picture of an image that depicts the devil with a pitchfork, horns, cape and sometimes dressed in red or black. This is the wrong image! If the devil actually appeared dressed like the images, we've seen over the years then we would be on high alert to know him when he appears before us. Nah, this joker shows up in your thoughts which may cause you to react in a way that pleases him. The devil likes it when we respond the way that makes him happy and he appears to have power over us.

I've read over the years and heard it repeated that freedom is not free. I would say that the price of freedom is definitely not free, nor is it cheap. There is real freedom and then there's a false sense of freedom. Have you ever experienced a frightening event in your life, even a scary movie with gory scenes and it frighten you for a moment and you said, I will never be frightened like that again? You decreed and declared to the world that I'll never be frightened like that ever. Then you watch the same or similar movie and find yourself covering your face in fright at the same gory scenes?

Ok, let's take it to real life situations, I have a close relative who had and still has a serious alcohol addiction. He's not living a life for Christ, but goes to church three times a year, C.M.E. (Christmas, Mother's Day and Easter). Last Easter he went to church and the pastor ask if there's anything in your life that's got you trapped or addicted and you want to be delivered from it, please come to the altar and we're going to pray. His family witnessed his desire to believe the pastor's declaration. He went to the altar, the pastor asked if he wanted to share what is his addition was and he said yes. He declared before God and the congregation that he was addicted to drinking alcohol for years. The pastor said repeat after me. "I, _____ have an alcohol drinking addiction" "I'm here today because I want to be delivered from this addiction, I believe you God to deliver me from this horrible sin. Because I believe you God, I no longer have an addiction Amen. He repeated it all. The entire Church celebrated. Since Easter, he has not stopped drinking alcohol and reminds us that the Pastor said he no longer has an alcohol addiction. He frequently says I can drink all I want because the Pastor confirmed my belief "I no longer have an alcohol addiction". He constantly repeats the pastor's declaration to the family, because his belief is in what the pastor said. He does what he wants to do and says what he wants us to accept. This is deception, a false sense of freedom. He's not free, freedom is not free for you to live a life unbecoming of Christ. Release and living in freedom must be taught and is a process to live and walk out. This goes back to living in confinement. He's still confined to his own thinking and the warden (the devil) reminds him that he's good where he is, so stay put and don't mess up your good behavior record with me. Having a good behavior record with the devil…. umm.

You may have or have not witnessed an experience where someone has been told by someone in a trusted place of authority that they're living in an 'ok' place in God, but you know that truthfully it is not a life pleasing to God. How should we approach a situation where we know that someone is confined, and they don't realize that they can be released and live a life pleasing to God? Do we reflect on an area and time in our own life in which we were confined and didn't know that we were confined, and God sent someone to us to walk with us to be delivered? We can't so easily forget that God delivered/released us so that we could help someone else. God has no other legs, arms, or mouthpieces except the ones He gave to us to use for His glory. How are you using your legs, arms and mouthpiece to glorify God and come alongside someone else to help them be released from confinement? When was the last time God said to you to share your testimony? There will be times, opportunities for us to share our testimony. Be mindful of what part of your testimony that God wants you to share. Sometimes, God will say share all of a particular testimony and then there will be times when God says to only share a portion of your testimony. Always follow God's leading in sharing. HE will never lead you wrong. We don't want to damage someone by oversharing. Trust God.

When we remember the Harriett Tubman story, where she didn't remain in freedom alone, but went back to get others so that they could enjoy freedom. It makes for great conversation and witnessing when we get together and talk about how we've been delivered and released from the confinement of the devil. It always ends up in a 'Thank You God' benediction. As you take a few minutes from reading this book, I encourage you to ask God to bring to your remembrance someone who needs to hear your testimony of being released from confinement so that they can believe God will do it for them as well. We should never want to live as an island and not give testimony to what our great big God did for us. I refer to Luke 22:31-32: And the Lord said, Simon, Simon, behold, Satan hath desired to have you, that he may sift you as wheat: But I have prayed for thee, that thy faith fail not: and when thou art converted, strengthen thy brethren.

There are still areas in my life where I am confined, and I need to make a conscious decision to allow God to have full control of these areas. I understand, there will always be areas that I have many questions about and may never get the answers (I want) but I must trust God greater to live in a state of peace and not struggle with getting answers.

Chapter Five

Why Release the Why

Let's take a look into the definition of Release. Release – to allow something to move, act or flow freely.

Experiences try to hold us hostage. Whether it's being handcuffed to a bad relationship, a divorce, miscarriage, personal drug addiction, rejection by parents, being adopted, abortion, spending time in jail, molestation, suicide, rape, drug addiction of a family member, mental and physical abuse, or loss of a loved one -- God can and wants to free us so we can live the abundant life He has for us. Have you ever wondered why we can vividly remember past uncomfortable experiences and play them back over and over in technicolor in our mind? It's because the enemy knows that if he can keep pressing the replay button in our mind, we'll spend time analyzing every segment of the playback and sink deeper and deeper into depression. Depression is REAL and I've been the victim of functioning in my depression. I would start my day reading the Our Daily Bread devotional, say a prayer, shower, get dress for the day and before I walked out of my bedroom, I'd practice my 'smile' for the day. This is not the place in the book where you get deep, LOL. Don't tell me that there haven't been times that you had to practice your smile before leaving the house for the day. I'd even practiced in the car before arriving to my destination. You've heard the cliché "fake it until you make it". Well I had the faking part on lock – but the making it was nowhere in sight. When I tried to look for the light at the end of the tunnel, it always ended up being a train that ran me over again and again. I had to fight to get out of bed because there were people that I had to interact with daily. I was afraid to be alone. I couldn't sit in one spot for more than five minutes. I had to be busy doing something, like finding something to clean or wash. I knew what was happening, but I couldn't get off the merry-go-round. The merry-go-round would speed up every time I thought I could get off - confinement. I attended church every Sunday because if I didn't show up, I'd get a text message asking,

"Where are you?" All my life I've never wanted to be singled out for bad or good deeds. So, I showed up to church. Here's what I'd tell myself, "today I'm going to the altar and surrender everything that's hurting me". Then I'd get to church and enjoy the service and convince myself that I was ok. I would deliberately speak to people who were known to be seers (prophets) hoping that they would SEE my pain. Yes, several people would ask 'how are you?' after the death of my sister, my momma and my husband and I'd kindly say, 'I'm ok' or 'I'm doing good' Yeah right, rush to my car and cry all the way home. That's not living – that's existing.

I write all of this to encourage you to take inventory of your heart, mind and spirit to evaluate the thoughts that the enemy has you replaying about your past that hold you in confinement. Those things that set you back to your original feelings and disappointments like they just happened. I may not have listed your particular issue but know that whatever that thing is that you can't seem to get free from needs to be faced with the help of God and HIS helpers. You deserve peace and joy and the way to it is to RELEASE!

Chapter Six

RELEASE

I desired to be free and knew that I had to move on what I desired. The first step I had to take, and it was one of the hardest things I've ever had to do in my life:

- Admit to myself that I wasn't healthy spiritually, mentally nor physically. 'Hi I'm Gladys and I'm afraid of my state of being'

  Then I had to ask God who I could trust to talk to that would be confidential and not celebrate that I wasn't healthy. (This may take some time, because the people who you think are confidential, may not be the one.)

I would talk to God and present my list of people who I thought were candidates, and the Lord would say 'not that one'. That person is confidential, but they can't carry the weight of knowing all that you need to release. Don't be alarmed if the Lord says NO to all of the people on YOUR list. I prayed and asked God to send the person that HE would choose for this time of my life, because I really wanted to be healthy and whole. I had to become open to HIS will not mind and accept HIS will and process. It was HARD. IT WILL BE HARD to take your hands off the control switch, but it's necessary if you wanted to live free.

I received a call from my very best friend of over 25 years, before I moved to

Hampton, VA, before I married Andrew Williams Sr. It was Jada Jackson, she simply said 'Henderson, you're not healthy and you need to see a Christian counselor, one who doesn't know you and you don't know them. Your insurance will pay for the visit, I need you to make the appointment and text me the appointment date and time'. She made me accountable to follow through because she knows me. I said OK, so she would hang-up the phone. Did I make the appointment right away? NO. I replayed her message over and over in my mind – does she REALLY think that I'm in need of professional counseling? She needs to leave me alone. She would text me and I wouldn't respond, she knows me and was not offended by my nonresponse. She text me a message that caused me to make the appointment 'Henderson, your life depends on you getting help, God has need of you and HE can't use you in the state you're in' - she was getting on my nerves, the last one I had. Then I had to take that next step:

- I called a Christian counseling service on a Monday afternoon. The receptionist was very kind and verified that my insurance would cover the session with at $15 co-pay. Then she said, everything is verified, and you can come tomorrow afternoon – silence – shock WHATTT??? TOMORROW??

  Who in the world gets a next day appointment? I was upset once again. I only called so that I could text Jada and tell her I had an appointment that was two weeks out. Yes, I'd told God that I wanted to be healthy spiritually, mentally and physically, BUT this train was moving tooooo fast.

The stigma of many Christians believers is that to see a counselor of any sort, was a sign that you didn't trust God. There is also a place called 'Christian Confinement

Jail Cell'. This is the jail cell that says, your loved one died five years ago, why are you still crying? Or, it's been six months since your loved one died, why aren't you crying all the time and looking sad, how dare you smile. You're divorced, get over it and move on you were only married for ten years. Then you don't openly cry in church, because the senior mother of the church didn't shed a tear when her child died. Stop all that crying about the rejection you experienced as a child, you're grown now. Here's one that was told to me three months after the death of my husband 'take them wedding rings off, you're not married because when my husband died, I took mine off immediately. You've gotta move on'. I really wish I could add an emoji that matched my facial expression after that exchange. The Christian Confinement Jail

Cell has caused a ton of issues for believers. If you've ever made a statement to someone who doesn't respond to instances that have occurred in their life the way you have responded, I beg of you to stop and just pray the Word over that individual. Please join me in tearing down the Christian Confinement Jail Cell that has caused people not to just leave church, but to leave God. Our places of worship should be a place of refuge providing a safe place to be healed. If you don't get anything else from this book, I want you to grab this nugget and spread it to the world 'IT'S OK' to get whatever help you need to be healthy spiritually, mentally and physically.

- I texted Jada and told her that I'd be seeing a Christian Counselor on the next day and she asked that I call her after the appointment – accountability. When I made the appointment, I specifically asked for an appointment not in my city – pride kicks in again.

- I went to the appointment, in another city, parked my car in front of the nutrition office just in case someone recognized my car, Christian Confine Jail Cell. My insides were shaking. What would I say, how long would the session take? Had my game-face on lock. I was glad that there was no one in the lobby but me.

- The counselor greeted me with a smile. My inside voice said 'she is smiling because she's about to get

paid. When she closed the door and said, 'I'm here to listen to you, hear your heart and pray with you not for you'. That's when I realized that this was a safe place and my Christian Confinement Jail Cell door was being opened. I explained why I was there because my friend insisted that I see a counselor. She said 'it is healthy to talk about what you're dealing with in a safe place' – confirmation of safe place. I began to 'unpack' the layers of issues that I was afraid to face head-on. The tears began to flow as I recalled my recent tragedy, death of my husband. The fear of being alone and feeling unprotected – no priest, no more provider, no protection. Admitting that you're not healthy is a step that you must take if you want to be healed. The hour long session went fast. It felt good to just know it was a safe place. The counselor recommended that I come back weekly for at least a month, I agreed. I texted Jada and told her about the appointment and she had the nerve to ask, 'when is your next appointment?' as usual, I didn't respond because it would mean that she was correct that I needed help. That feeling lasted until I got home and walked in my bedroom and the enemy was back on his job saying 'seeing a counselor it not of God. Someone at church probably saw you going in that office and they're going to tell leadership and membership that you're

unstable' – the fight was on! Choosing if I want to be healthy or literally die of stress with pain.

- I made the decision to attend counseling for the next four weeks. During this season of my life, I couldn't pray for myself, I would read the Word but nothing was sticking or making me feel any better. God encouraged me to share with my Prayer Partner/Sister Gail that I had started Christian counseling and her response was 'I'm so glad you're going, this will keep you from laying down in the intersection of Mercury Blvd and

Coliseum Drive at 5pm on Friday (one of the busiest intersection in Hampton, VA). Whew! God said that she would pray for me without conviction of my decision. So now two people knew that I was getting healthy. She would track my visits and ensure that I didn't find any excuse not to attend the appointment. I could only share with those who God said too. Over time, God allowed me to share with others, I won't put them on blast.

While attending my week counseling session, I discovered so many things about my past that I'd hidden away, even from my childhood. I was given a safe place to unpack childhood, teen-hood, young adult-hood, young adult parent-hood, relationship-hood, marriage-hood, disappointment-hood, death of loved ones–hood and so many more hurts. I exposed how I didn't want to live and how I'd ask God each night to forgive me of my sins and to please come get me while I slept. Then I would wake up the next morning and fuss at God for not honoring my request. I kept going, I kept on going to counseling until I could pray for myself and not be afraid to be alone with my thoughts. It was a fight of great proportion that I faced each day.

There are still days that the enemy plays back those dark days that I came out of, but the amazing comfort is the sting of remembering the past is no longer painful. Do I miss my loved ones, YES? I still cry, I still talk to them – even fuss at them for leaving me. Do I grieve bad decisions I've made in the past? I remember them, and I also remember that God has forgiven me of those bad decisions, so I smile and tell God thanks and tell the enemy to take his comments to God. I am forgiven – repeat this as many times as you need too. Your deliverance is crucial – I had to make myself face the fears that I had been living with in hiding. Let's get to the other side of this season together in victory.

Today, I've surrounded myself with people who will pray for me and want the best things for me. I have a couple more people who hold me accountable for remaining healthy spiritually, mentally and physically. These individuals know who they are and how much I value them being in my life. Yes, I'm still a private person, but willing to share my testimony with those who are fearful of asking for professional help. I've fallen in love with me and desire the best for me. I don't walk in fear of openly seeking help for any area of my life. You owe it to God and yourself to be healthy, spiritually, mentally and physically.

I encourage you to surround yourself with people who want to see you grow, hold you accountable in love, walk with you when you want to give up, let your cry and vent and still love you the next day. Fight through the fear of not being respected tomorrow if I share my heart. Fear is a bondage holder as well.

Give God the best **<u>YOU</u>** that He created.

Acknowledgements

I don't know where to start because I've been blessed with a long list of great people that have stood by my side and held my arms high so that I could win. I believe the only things that really change your life are the experiences you live through and the people God bring into your life. I'm blessed with some amazing people whom I've shared life with and received great knowledge from. It's going to be impossible to thank everybody who's helped me, and it would take a couple chapters! I'll try my best.

My parents, Rev. Paul and Mrs. Iola have played the key roles in my success. They gave me love, guidance, structure, and discipline that would mold me into the Godly woman that I am today. I'm eternally grateful to them for the ultimate gift of keeping God first in my life. Thanks momma and daddy – love and miss you both.

To my sisters, Ruth and Dorothy (deceased), along with my baby sister Inez Ann thanks for your love and support. To explain the depth, love, and support that my spiritual sisters have given would be to write a fifty-page book alone – you know who you are! God sent me a big brother, Cornell Von Jordan, with a very similar testimony of a spouse transitioning shortly after my Andrew. We fuss like siblings, cry together then find a good restaurant to go eat. Mentors are treasured, to my sister, confidant, mentor, and sand-paper cousin, Bishop Ruby Lee Johnson Pedescleaux, God always lets you know when to call me.

To my children, I would not be where I am today without your love, support and encouragement. You've wiped my tears, gave me lots to smile about, wouldn't let me give up, insisted that I continue to fight to live and taught me perseverance. I know that I'll forget someone, please charge it to my head and not to my heart – here goes. Neco, Tina, Rekinna, Tatanashe and Carlos, Jai-Keith and Kentichia, Andrew Jr., Aja and Derrick, Rodney, Robbie, Fred and Vernell, Marqueese and Anita, Marcus and Crystal, Ivan and Jackie, Calandra, Bernard and Shirl, Keith and Deidre, Duane and Tiffany, Kerita and…

To my grandchildren, great grandchildren, nieces', great nieces', nephews, great nephews know that you have my heart. I love you more than you could ever imagine.

There have been many people who have impacted my life and success along the way and I sincerely appreciate every one of you.

I call you 'My Village' because I have villagers that span the globe not just in the United States of America. My extended family across the world, my church family, Cornerstone Worship Center International Inc., my Professional career co-workers, friends, mentors, and my hometown heroes thank you from the bottom of my heart for your belief in me – I will never outgrow home.

One Last Thing

May I ask you for a favor?

If you got anything this this book, if you took notes, if it shifted your thinking or inspired you at all, I'm hoping you'll do something for me.

Give a copy to somebody else.

Ask them to read it. Let them know what's possible for them if they begin to release their WHY.

Thank You.

For speaking engagement, workshop facilitator, business coaching and book publishing assistance, please send request to

Manifest Destiny LLC

c/o Gail Taylor

2019 Cunningham Drive, Suite 416, Hampton, VA 23666

(757) 726-7249 or (757) 915-6677

manifestdestinyllc3@gmail.com